I0415799

January 2012

CREDIT RATING AGENCIES

Alternative Compensation Models for Nationally Recognized Statistical Rating Organizations

GAO

Accountability * Integrity * Reliability

CREDIT RATING AGENCIES

Alternative Compensation Models for Nationally Recognized Statistical Rating Organizations

Highlights of GAO-12-240, a report to congressional committees

Why GAO Did This Study

Over the past decade, concerns repeatedly have been raised about the accuracy of credit ratings provided by a number of nationally recognized statistical rating organizations (NRSRO). NRSRO critics often point to the conflict of interest created by the industry's predominant compensation model in which issuers of securities pay the rating agencies for their ratings (issuer-pays model). In 2006, Congress established Securities and Exchange Commission (SEC) oversight over NRSROs, and recently enhanced this authority through the Dodd-Frank Wall Street Reform and Consumer Protection Act (Dodd-Frank Act). This act also requires GAO to study alternative means for compensating NRSROs. This report discusses (1) alternative models for compensating NRSROs and (2) SEC's actions to implement the act's requirements specific to its oversight of NRSROs. To do this work, GAO leveraged its 2010 report on NRSROs (GAO-10-782), reviewed comment letters submitted to SEC as part of its study of alternative compensation models, proposed and finalized rules issued under the act; and interviewed SEC staff and authors of alternative compensation models.

What GAO Recommends

SEC should consult with the authors of the proposed models to obtain all available information as it considers the various alternative compensation models and any recommendations for statutory changes SEC determines should be made to implement the findings of its section 939F study. SEC agreed with the recommendation.

View GAO-12-240 and components.
For more information, contact A. Nicole Clowers at (202) 512-8678 or clowersa@gao.gov.

What GAO Found

As of January 2012, GAO identified seven alternative models for compensating NRSROs (see table below). These models generally were designed to address the conflict of interest in the issuer-pays model, better align the NRSROs' interest with users of ratings, or improve incentives NRSROs have to produce reliable and high-quality ratings. However, the amount of detail currently available for each model varies and none has been implemented. According to some of the authors of the models, there is little incentive to continue developing these models because it appears unlikely they will receive attention from regulators or legislators. For example, these authors noted that SEC had not reached out to them to further discuss these models as part of its ongoing study of alternative compensation models for credit rating agencies.

Identified Alternative Compensation Models for NRSROs

Name	Description
Random selection	Issuers continue to pay for ratings but payment is made to a ratings board that randomly assigns NRSROs to rate issuances.
Investor-owned	Institutional investors create and operate an NRSRO. Issuers are required to get two ratings, one from the investor-owned NRSRO and one from an NRSRO of their choice.
Stand-alone	NRSROs choose which issues to rate. A transaction fee for original issuance and fees from secondary market transactions pay for the ratings.
Designation	NRSROs choose which issues to rate and securities holders designate which NRSRO(s) would receive the fees they pay for rating(s). A third party collects and distributes fees.
User-pays	Third-party auditors determine who is "using" ratings and require that all "users" pay the NRSROs.
Alternative user-pays	Creditors' resources are pooled and a government agency or independent board uses these resources to solicit ratings. NRSROs bid on the right to rate products.
Issuer and investor-pays	Issuers and investors pay a fee on the issuance of new debt and secondary market trades. NRSROs are placed in a continuous queue and assigned to rate issues as their number comes up. Assignment eventually is based on an NRSRO's performance.

Source: GAO summary of alternative compensation models.

During debate on the Dodd-Frank Act, a model similar to the random-selection model was proposed through an amendment that would have added a section 15E(w) to the Securities Exchange Act of 1934 (15E(w) model). Although the amendment was not included in the final legislation, section 939F of the Dodd-Frank Act requires SEC to study, among other things, alternative means for compensating NRSROs. It also authorizes SEC to, upon completion of the study, establish by rule a system for assigning NRSROs to determine initial credit ratings and monitor the ratings of structured finance products in a manner that prevents the arranger from selecting the NRSRO that will determine the credit rating should SEC conclude that an alternative system is necessary or appropriate. In issuing any rule, SEC also must give thorough consideration to the section 15E(w) model and implement the model unless it determines that an alternative would better serve the public interest and protect investors. As part of its solicitation of comments for its ongoing study of alternative compensation models, SEC requested that interested parties use the framework GAO developed in the 2010 report on NRSROs to evaluate the section 15E(w) and other models. GAO created this evaluative framework to help identify the relative strengths and weaknesses and potential trade offs (in terms of policy goals) of the models (see table below). Based on GAO's analysis of comment letters to SEC, while a number of comment letters generally favored implementing the section 15E(w) model, slightly more opposed the implementation of any of the models. Those supporting the 15E(w) model highlighted the need to address the conflict of interests inherent in the issuer-pays model. Those opposed to the alternative compensation models cited concerns of replacing one set of conflicts of interest with another and the costs of implementation. A number of the letters either supported or made suggestions for improving existing SEC rules. A few comment letters also raised legal questions about the implementation or rulemaking for specific aspects of certain models.

In addition to studying alternative compensation models, SEC has begun to implement a number of Dodd-Frank Act requirements pertaining to NRSROs. These requirements include additional rulemakings related to NRSROs' disclosures of performance statistics, credit ratings methodologies, third-party due diligence for asset-backed securities, and analyst training and testing standards. Of nine rulemaking requirements, SEC has adopted three final rules that implement all or part of certain requirements and proposed rules for the remaining requirements. SEC also has been working to establish an Office of Credit Ratings

as required by the act. Moreover, SEC examination staff completed the first cycle of annual examinations of each NRSRO as required by the Dodd-Frank Act and published their summary report in September 2011. As part of its study on alternative compensation models for NRSROs, SEC solicited comment on SEC's authority to implement various alternative compensation models. According to SEC staff, they are reviewing the comment letters received and evaluating authority issues. Any recommendations for regulatory or statutory changes SEC determines should be made to implement the findings of the study are to be included in their report to Congress, due in July 2012. The model authors' opinions of the extent to which statutory changes would be needed to implement their alternative compensation models vary, with one stating that current law provides SEC with the necessary authority and another anticipating the need for legislation. Given that NRSROs continue to primarily use the issuer-pays, and to a lesser extent, the subscriber-pays models, the use of any alternative model or models would likely have to be at the direction of SEC or Congress. However, the extent to which SEC's existing authorities would allow it to implement any of the alternative models by rule largely will depend on the alternative model or models selected. Obtaining as complete information on the models as available, such as by consulting with the models' authors, will be important for SEC to fully assess each model in order to make its decision and any recommendations for statutory changes SEC determines should be made to implement the findings of its section 939Fstudy.

Framework for Evaluating Alternative Models for Compensating NRSROs

Factors	Description
✓ Independence	The ability for the compensation model to mitigate conflicts of interest inherent between the entity paying for the rating and the NRSRO. Key questions include: What potential conflicts of interest exist in the alternative compensation model and what controls, if any, would need to be implemented to mitigate these conflicts?
✓ Accountability	The ability of the compensation model to promote NRSROs' responsibility for the accuracy and timeliness of their ratings. Key questions include: How does the compensation model create economic incentives for NRSROs to produce quality ratings over the life of an issuance? How is NRSRO performance evaluated and by whom?
✓ Competition	The extent to which the compensation model creates an environment in which NRSROs compete for customers by producing higher-quality ratings at competitive prices. Key questions include: To what extent does the compensation model encourage competition around the quality of ratings, ratings fees, and product innovation? To what extent does it allow for flexibility in the differing sizes, resources, and specialties of NRSROs?
✓ Transparency	The accessibility, usability, and clarity of the compensation model and the dissemination of information on the model to market participants. Key questions include: How transparent are the model's processes and procedures for determining ratings fees and compensating NRSROs? How would NRSROs obtain ratings business?
✓ Feasibility	The simplicity and ease with which the compensation model can be implemented in the securities market. Key questions include: What are the costs to implement the compensation model and who would fund them? Who would administer the compensation model? What, if any, infrastructure would be needed to implement it?
✓ Market acceptance and choice	The willingness of the securities market to accept the compensation model, the ratings produced under that model, and any new market players established by the compensation model. Key questions include: What role do market participants have in selecting NRSROs to produce ratings, assessing the quality of ratings, and determining NRSRO compensation?
✓ Oversight	The evaluation of the model to ensure it works as intended. Key questions include: Does the model provide for an independent internal control function? What external oversight does the compensation model provide to ensure it is working as intended?

Source: GAO.

Contents

Abbreviations

CRARA	Credit Rating Agency Reform Act of 2006
Dodd-Frank Act	Dodd-Frank Wall Street Reform and Consumer Protection Act
MSRB	Municipal Securities Rulemaking Board
NRSRO	nationally recognized statistical rating organization
OCIE	Office of Compliance Inspections and Examinations
SEC	Securities and Exchange Commission

United States Government Accountability Office
Washington, DC 20548

January 18, 2012

The Honorable Tim Johnson
Chairman
The Honorable Richard C. Shelby
Ranking Member
Committee on Banking, Housing,
    and Urban Affairs
United States Senate

The Honorable Spencer Bachus
Chairman
The Honorable Barney Frank
Ranking Member
Committee on Financial Services
House of Representatives

As the financial crisis unfolded in 2007 and 2008, questions were raised about the role that nationally recognized statistical rating organizations (NRSRO) played in the securitization of high-risk mortgages into investment grade securities, the accuracy of the credit ratings assigned to these securities, and the integrity of these NRSROs' ratings process. Although ratings downgrades for investment grade securities are generally infrequent, a report by the Permanent Investigations Subcommittee of the Senate Homeland Security and Governmental Affairs Committee notes that by 2010, 90 percent of the residential mortgage-backed securities issued in 2006 and 2007 that had received an investment grade rating from the two largest NRSROs were downgraded to junk bond status.[1] Critics of NRSROs pointed to the conflict of interest created by the industry's predominant compensation model in which issuers of securities pay the rating agencies for their ratings (issuer-pays model) as a contributing factor to the poor ratings performance.

Moreover, in the early 2000s, the NRSROs were criticized for failing to warn investors in a timely manner about the impending bankruptcies of

---

[1] Staff of Permanent Subcommittee on Investigations, Committee on Homeland Security and Governmental Affairs, 112th Congress, *Wall Street and the Financial Crisis: Anatomy of a Financial Collapse*, 263-267 (2011).

Enron and other issuers. Consequently, Congress required the Securities and Exchange Commission (SEC) to study the role and function of credit rating agencies in the securities markets.[2] In its 2003 report, SEC identified multiple concerns, such as the concentration of credit rating agencies, the potential conflict of interest generated by the NRSROs' issuer-pays compensation model, and the lack of a formal regulatory program to oversee NRSROs.[3]

To address these and other concerns, Congress passed the Credit Rating Agency Reform Act of 2006 (CRARA), which established SEC oversight over credit rating agencies registered as NRSROs.[4] In February and November 2009, SEC amended some of its initial NRSRO rules and issued additional rules intended to enhance NRSRO disclosures of performance-related data to investors, strengthen the integrity of the ratings process, and more effectively address the potential for conflicts of interest. SEC also held a roundtable relating to its oversight of credit rating agencies in April 2009, at which participants expressed concerns about, among other things, market concentration, and discussed proposed alternative means for compensating rating agencies that could

---

[2]In 2003 only three credit rating agencies were identified as NRSROs by SEC staff. Currently, there are nine credit rating agencies registered as NRSROs with SEC.

[3]See SEC, *Report on the Role and Function of Credit Rating Agencies in the Operation of the Securities Markets, As Required by Section 702(b) of the Sarbanes-Oxley Act of 2002* (Washington, D.C.: Jan. 24, 2003). The practice of issuers paying for their ratings could create a conflict of interest. Arguably, the dependence of rating agencies on revenues from the companies they rate could induce them to rate issuers more liberally, and temper their diligence in probing for negative information. Furthermore, the rating agencies' practice of charging fees based on the size of the issuance could exacerbate potential conflicts because large issuers could inordinately influence the agencies.

[4]Pub. L. No. 109-291, 120 Stat. 1327 (2006) (amending the Securities Exchange Act of 1934 and codified at various sections of Title 15 of the U.S. Code).

reduce conflicts of interest and ways to increase NRSRO incentives to produce accurate ratings.[5]

More recently, the Dodd-Frank Wall Street Reform and Consumer Protection Act (Dodd-Frank Act) imposed new self-executing requirements on NRSROs, required SEC to adopt certain rules for NRSROs, and required SEC to conduct certain studies.[6] For example, SEC must periodically review the implementation of policies that NRSROs must establish concerning evaluations of possible conflicts of interest related to former employees. Other requirements relate to disclosures of performance statistics, credit ratings methodologies, third-party due diligence for asset-backed securities, and analyst training and testing standards. In addition, section 939F requires SEC to study, among other things, the credit rating process for structured finance products and associated conflicts of interest, the feasibility of establishing a system in which a public or private utility or a self-regulatory organization assigns NRSROs to determine the credit ratings of structured finance products, and alternative means for compensating NRSROs that would create incentives for accurate credit ratings (hereafter referred to as the 939F study). Section 939F requires SEC to submit to Congress the findings of the study and any recommendations for regulatory or statutory changes SEC determines should be made to implement the findings by July 21, 2012.

The Dodd-Frank Act also requires us to study alternative means for compensating NRSROs (alternative compensation models), including any

---

[5]Subsequent to the SEC roundtable, we also discussed alternative compensation models, see GAO, *Securities and Exchange Commission: Action Needed to Improve Rating Agency Registration Program and Performance Related Disclosures*, GAO-10-782 (Washington, D.C.: Sept. 22, 2010). We issued the report in response to a mandate in CRARA. The report identified and described five alternative compensation models and provided an evaluative framework for assessing the models. In addition, the report examined how SEC implemented CRARA and the impact of SEC's rules promulgated under CRARA on the quality of credit ratings, financial markets, competition in the credit rating industry, and the process for NRSRO registration.

[6]Pub. L. No. 111-203, §§ 931-939H, 872 Stat 1376, 1872-1890 (2010). In addition to provisions related to oversight, the Dodd-Frank Act requires every federal agency to review regulations that require assessments of the creditworthiness of a security or money market instrument and any references to credit ratings in such regulations; to modify such regulations to remove any reference to, or requirement for, reliance on credit ratings; and substitute a standard of creditworthiness an agency deems appropriate. 15 U.S.C. § 78o-7 note.

statutory changes that would facilitate the use of such an alternative model.[7] In response to this mandate, this report discusses (1) alternative compensation models for NRSROs and (2) the actions SEC has taken to implement the Dodd-Frank Act requirements specific to SEC's oversight of NRSROs and SEC's authority to implement an alternative compensation model under current securities laws.

To identify alternative compensation models, we conducted a literature search to identify academic, industry papers, or journal articles and we reviewed past GAO reports, notably our 2010 report that examined alternative compensation models, among other things.[8] We also reviewed the comment letters submitted to SEC for the 939F study. We reviewed these letters to identify market participants' views on the implementation of an alternative compensation model and, where possible, the perceived advantages and disadvantages of the models. In addition, we interviewed SEC staff and the authors of the compensation models discussed in our 2010 report to identify any new models and obtain information on any additional work they have completed on the previously identified models. We also solicited and obtained comments from the authors of the two models we identified since we issued the 2010 report. To identify the actions SEC has taken to implement various Dodd-Frank Act requirements, we reviewed SEC proposed and final rules issued pursuant to the act and interviewed SEC staff to identify prior and current regulatory actions that SEC has taken and challenges it has faced in implementing the requirements. To review SEC's authority to implement alternative compensation models and statutory changes that would facilitate the use of an alternative means of compensation, we interviewed SEC staff and attorneys, reviewed the comment letters submitted to SEC for its 939F study, reviewed relevant statutory authority, and solicited comments from the authors of the compensation models, which included two law professors, an economist, and market participants.

We conducted this performance audit from July 2011 to January 2012 in accordance with all generally accepted government auditing standards. Those standards require that we plan and perform the audit to obtain sufficient, appropriate evidence to provide a reasonable basis for our findings and conclusions based on our audit objectives. We believe that

---

[7]Pub. L. No 111-203, tit. IX, § 939D, 124 Stat. 1376, 1888 (2010).

[8]GAO-10-782.

evidence obtained provides a reasonable basis for our findings and conclusions based on our audit objectives.

Background

A credit rating is an assessment of the creditworthiness of an obligor as an entity or in relation to specific securities or money market instruments.[9] SEC first used the term "Nationally Recognized Statistical Rating Organization" in 1975 to describe those rating agencies whose ratings could be relied upon to determine capital charges for different types of debt securities (securities) broker-dealers held.[10] Since then, SEC has used the NRSRO designation in a number of regulations, and the term has been embedded in numerous federal and state laws and regulations, investment guidelines, and private contracts. As will be discussed, SEC has issued a series of proposals regarding the removal of references to credit ratings in its regulations in accordance with the Dodd-Frank Act.

NRSRO credit ratings are intended to measure the likelihood of default for an issue or issuer, although some also measure variables such as the expected value of dollar losses given a default. The NRSROs describe ratings as being intended only to reflect credit risk, not other valuation factors such as liquidity or price risk. To determine an appropriate rating, analysts at rating agencies use publicly available information and market and economic data, and may hold discussions and obtain nonpublic information from the issuer.

[9]Section 3(a)(60) of the Securities Exchange Act of 1934 (codified at 15 U.S.C. § 78c(a)(60)).

[10]17 C.F.R. § 240.15c3-1. Rule 15c3-1, also known as the net capital rule, establishes minimum regulatory capital requirements for broker-dealers. A broker-dealer calculates its actual net capital by subtracting prescribed percentages of the market value of its securities, known as a haircut, to discount for potential market movements. The net capital rule imposes a lower haircut for certain securities that are rated in higher ratings categories by NRSROs. The net capital rule also refers to NRSRO ratings in connection with the capital treatment of certain currency options, and the calculation of counterparty risk for broker-dealers and over-the-counter derivatives dealers under certain circumstances. In accordance with the he Dodd-Frank Act, in April 2011, SEC proposed regulations to remove from the net capital rule all references to credit ratings and to substitute an alternative standard of creditworthiness. SEC generally proposes that a broker-dealer take a 15 percent haircut on its proprietary positions in commercial paper, nonconvertible debt, and preferred stock unless the broker-dealer has a process for determining creditworthiness that satisfies certain criteria. SEC also proposes to remove references to NRSRO ratings from other rule provisions. *See Removal of Certain References to Credit Ratings Under the Securities Exchange Act of 1934,* 76 Fed. Reg. 26550 (May 6, 2011).

Issuers seek credit ratings for reasons such as improving the marketability or pricing of their securities or satisfying investors, lenders, or counterparties. Institutional investors, such as mutual funds, pension funds, and insurance companies, are among the largest owners of debt securities in the United States and are substantial users of credit ratings. Institutional investors may use credit ratings as one of several inputs to their internal credit assessments and investment analyses, or to identify pricing discrepancies for their trading operations. Broker-dealers also use ratings to recommend and sell securities to their clients or determine acceptable counterparties, and collateral levels for outstanding credit exposures.

CRARA established SEC oversight of credit rating agencies registered as NRSROs. Specifically, CRARA added section 15E to the Securities Exchange Act of 1934 to provide SEC with examination authority and establish a registration program for credit rating agencies seeking NRSRO designation. SEC adopted final rules for a formal registration and oversight program for NRSROs in June 2007.[11] SEC amended several of these rules in February and December 2009 with the goal of further increasing transparency of NRSRO rating methodologies, strengthening the disclosures of ratings performance, prohibiting NRSROs from engaging in certain practices, and enhancing NRSRO record keeping.[12]

Since the implementation of CRARA, SEC has registered 10 credit rating agencies as NRSROs. One of these credit rating agencies has recently

---

[11]*Oversight of Credit Rating Agencies Registered as Nationally Recognized Statistical Rating Organizations,* 72 Fed. Reg. 33564, 33619-36 (June 18, 2007).(Final Rule).(codified, as amended, at 17 C.F.R. §§ 240.17g-1 – 240.17g-6 and 17 C.F.R. § 249b.300) (2010).

[12]*Amendments to Rules for Nationally Recognized Statistical Rating Organizations,* 74 Fed. Reg. 6456 (Feb. 2, 2009). (Amending 17 C.F.R. §§ 240.17g-2, 240.17g-3, 240.17g-5 and Form NRSRO); *Amendments to Rules for Nationally Recognized Statistical Rating Organizations,* 74 Fed and Reg. 63833 (Dec. 4. 2009).(Amending 17 C.F.R. §§ 240.17g-2, 240.17g-5 and 243.100). In December 2009, SEC proposed rules that would require NRSRO compliance officers to furnish an annual report to SEC, disclose additional information about sources of revenues on Form NRSRO, and make publicly available a consolidated report containing information about revenues of the NRSRO attributable to persons paying the NRSRO for the issuance or maintenance of a credit rating. *Proposed Rules for Nationally Recognized Statistical Rating Organizations,* 74 Fed. Reg. 63866 (Dec. 4, 2009). (Proposed amendments to 17 C.F.R. §§ 240.17g-3, 249b.300 and Form NRSRO and proposed new § 240.17g-7).

withdrawn from registration as an NRSRO.[13] Six NRSROs use the issuer-pays compensation model and three operate primarily under the subscriber-pays compensation model, in which users pay a subscription fee to the NRSRO for access to its ratings. Despite the growth in the number of NRSROs and the availability of credit ratings from NRSROs operating under a subscriber-pays model, the market remains highly concentrated. In 2011, SEC reported that the three largest NRSROs (Standard & Poor's, Moody's Investment Services, and Fitch Ratings) issued approximately 97 percent of all outstanding ratings. Furthermore, NRSROs operating under the issuer-pays model issued approximately 99 percent of the total currently outstanding NRSRO credit ratings. Economists note that the credit rating industry has exhibited a high level of concentration throughout much of its history. SEC and others have noted that the regulatory use of ratings, economies of scale, high fixed costs, and network effects (the value or utility of products or services increasing with the number of users) as factors that have created barriers to entry and led to concentration in the credit rating industry.

New Developments on Alternative Compensation Models Are Limited

In our 2010 report, we identified five proposed models—random selection, investor-owned credit rating agency, stand-alone, designation, user-pays—and summarized key features of these proposed models.[14] When we conducted our 2010 study, the level of development for each model varied and none had been implemented. Our current study identified two additional proposed models—the alternative user-pays model and the issuer and investor-pays model—and found that little additional work had been completed on the previously identified models that would provide further details about how each would function. According to some of the authors of these models, there is little incentive to continue developing these models, as the issue of alternative compensation models for NRSROs and their possible implementation appears unlikely to receive much, if any, attention from regulators or legislators. For example, these authors told us that SEC had not reached out to them to further discuss these models as part of the 939F

---

[13]On October 13, 2011, Rating and Investment Information, Inc., which had been registered with SEC as an NRSRO since September 24, 2007, furnished SEC with a notice of withdrawal from registration as an NRSRO. The withdrawal became effective on November 27, 2011. See http://www.sec.gov/news/digest/2011/dig112811.htm.

[14]For more information about how we identified the alternative compensation models, see GAO-10-782.

study. However, SEC did solicit public comments about the models through a public notice in conducting its 939F study. Furthermore, SEC staff said that they held follow-up discussions with the authors of some of the models after the 2009 SEC roundtable.[15] While these models generally are intended to address the conflict of interest in the issuer-pays model, some comment letters to SEC for its section 939F study described a number of perceived disadvantages of these models. None of the models has been implemented as of January 2012.

Proposed Alternative Compensation Models

As of January 2012, we have identified seven proposed alternative compensation models. The following summarizes the key features of each of these proposed models.

Random Selection Model

A ratings clearinghouse randomly would select NRSROs to rate a new issuance in this proposed model. The clearinghouse could be a nonprofit, a governmental agency such as SEC, or a private-public partnership that would design the criteria by which new entrants could qualify as a credit rating agency. All issuers or sponsors that wanted ratings for their issuances would request them from the clearinghouse, which would use a random number generator to assign an NRSRO registered in the relevant asset class to produce the rating. The clearinghouse would notify the NRSRO of the opportunity to rate the issuance and provide basic information on the type of issuance but not the issuer's name. Not until the NRSRO agreed to complete the rating would the clearinghouse identify the issuer and details of the issuance. If the selected NRSRO agreed to rate the issuance, the issuer would pay a fee to the clearinghouse. The issuer also would pay to cover clearinghouse costs on top of those required to rate the security. Upon completion of the initial and maintenance ratings, the clearinghouse would distribute the fees to the NRSRO. The clearinghouse would set the ratings fees for the NRSRO depending on the type of security issued, but the letter rating would be free of charge to the public.

The proposed model incorporates a peer comparison review to create an incentive for NRSROs to produce quality ratings. As part of this review, the clearinghouse would evaluate the performance of all NRSROs on the

---

[15]Only one of the model authors submitted a comment letter to SEC for this study and none of the authors of the models we identified in our 2010 report submitted a comment letter.

basis of two empirical tests. For instance, if the default percentage of debt instruments rated by a given NRSRO differed from the default percentage of its peers by a set parameter, then the NRSRO would be subject to sanctions such as losing a percentage of business or rating fees. A second test would compare annual yields of identically rated debt securities from different asset classes. Securities in different asset classes that are rated similarly should have the same yield. An NRSRO would be subject to sanctions if the yields of identically rated securities differed by a certain threshold.

According to the author of this proposed model, by eliminating the linkage between the NRSRO and the issuer, this model would eliminate the conflict of interest stemming from the issuer-pays model. Furthermore, the author stated that the peer comparison review coupled with economic sanctions for poor performance would motivate the NRSROs to continually adjust their models and produce quality ratings.

Investor-Owned Credit Rating Agency Model

Under this model, sophisticated investors—referred to as "highly sophisticated institutional purchasers" in the model—would create and operate an NRSRO that would produce ratings. Issuers would have to obtain two ratings—one from the investor-owned NRSRO and the second from their choice of NRSRO. More specifically, an NRSRO could not publicly release a rating for which an issuer or sponsor paid unless the NRSRO received written notification that the issuer had paid an investor-owned NRSRO to publicly release its rating. The investor-owned NRSRO would publish its rating on or before the date on which the solicited NRSRO published its rating.

Institutional investors would have to qualify as highly sophisticated institutional purchasers before forming or joining an investor-owned agency. To qualify, an institutional investor would have to demonstrate that it was large and sophisticated, managed billions of dollars in assets, and could be relied upon to represent the buy-side interest in accurately rating debt market instruments. The investor-purchasers would hold majority voting and operational control over the agency, which could be for-profit or not-for-profit. Market forces would set the agency fees, which likely would be comparable to fees currently charged by dominant NRSROs. The letter rating and the underlying research would be free to the public.

Proponents of this model believe that it would improve the rating process by changing incentive structures. They said that investor-owned agencies would introduce new competition to the industry and balance the investors' interests against issuers' interests.

Stand-Alone Model

NRSROs would only be permitted to produce credit ratings in this proposed model. They could interact with and advise organizations being rated, but could not charge fees for advice.[16] Instead of receiving issuer fees, the NRSROs would be compensated through transaction fees for original issuance and secondary market transactions. The issuer or secondary-market seller would pay part of the fee, and the investor purchasing the security (in the primary or secondary market) would pay the other part. The NRSRO would be compensated over the life of the security based on these transaction fees. The letter rating would be free to the public.

Proponents of this model believe that by creating a funding source beyond the influence of both issuers and investors, NRSROs would focus on producing the most accurate and timely credit analysis rather than on satisfying the desires of any other vested interest.

Designation Model

In this proposed model, all NRSROs could opt to rate a new issuance and security holders would direct, or designate, fees to the NRSROs of their choice. When an issuer brought a security to market, it would have to provide all interested NRSROs with the information to rate the issuance and pay rating fees to a third-party administrator, which would manage the designation process.[17] The investors that purchased the debt issuance would each designate one or several NRSROs that rated the security to receive fees, based on their perception of research underlying the ratings. The third-party administrator would disburse the fees in accordance with the designations.[18] After the initial rating, the issuer would continue to pay maintenance rating fees to the third-party administrator. A final rating fee would be paid in conjunction with the

---

[16]If the NRSRO was part of a larger company, interaction between the parent company and the NRSRO would be prohibited.

[17]The model as proposed did not specify how ratings fees would be determined, but suggested that issuers could negotiate with the NRSROs to determine the fee or the NRSROs could establish a schedule for different kinds of securities.

[18]The proposed model suggests that the issuer's transfer agent could perform the responsibilities of the third-party administrator. The transfer agent currently is responsible for maintaining ownership records of security holders.

GAO-12-240 Credit Rating Agencies

retirement (or repurchase) of the security. The letter rating would be free to the public, while the research underlying it would be distributed to security holders and (at the discretion of the relevant NRSROs) to potential security holders.

The authors of this proposed model said it would eliminate conflicts of interest resulting from issuers paying for ratings and increase competition by allowing all NRSROs access to the information necessary to rate any issuance. The authors also stated that this model encourages NRSROs to prepare ratings because each NRSRO that did could profit from its ratings to the extent investors or other users find the ratings useful.

User-Pays Model

Issuers would not pay for ratings under this proposed model; rather, all users of ratings would enter into a contract with an NRSRO and pay for rating services. The proposal defines "user" as any entity that included a rated security, loan, or contract as an element of its assets or liabilities as recorded in an audited financial statement. For example, users could be holders of long or short positions in a fixed-income instrument, parties that refer to a credit rating in contractual commitments (that is, as parties to a lease), or parties to derivative products that rely on rated securities or entities. A user would have to pay for ratings services supplied during each period in which it booked the related asset or liability.

The proposed model relies on third-party auditors to ensure that NRSROs receive payment for their services from users of ratings. The user would have to demonstrate to the auditors that the holder of a rated instrument or contract paid for the rating services. Until auditors were satisfied that NRSROs had been properly compensated, they would not issue audit opinions. The model would require the close cooperation of the auditing community and the Public Company Auditing Oversight Board.[19]

The authors of this model stated that, while more cumbersome, the model attempts to capture "free riders"—those users of ratings that do not compensate NRSROs for the use of their intellectual property—and requires them to pay for ratings.

---

[19]The Public Company Accounting Oversight Board is a nonprofit corporation established by Congress to oversee the audits of public companies.

Alternative User-Pays Model	The alternative user-pays model would pool creditors' resources to secure ratings before debt was issued. A government agency or independent board would administer a user-fee system financed by debt purchasers, which would fund a competitive bidding process for the selection of rating agencies. The agency or board would solicit ratings before the debt issuance and then pay for the expense and related administrative costs through the user fee.[20] The user fee could be assessed through a flat fraction of a percentage fee on the initial purchasers of debt offerings. The user fee would allow the agency or board to finance initial ratings on a rolling basis, with the ratings for a given debt issuance being secured before the issuance of the debt. Although the fee could be assessed in many ways, the author of the model suggests a one-time fee at initial sale for administrative ease.

NRSROs would bid on the right to issue ratings with the agency or board determining how best to judge the bids and award the right to rate the issuance. For example, the agency or board could weigh factors such as price, extent of diligence the NRSRO proposed to undertake, and the disclosures the NRSRO would demand from issuers as a condition for the rating. The author believes the bidding process would serve to contain the costs for ratings through price competition, level the playing field for smaller competitors and new entrants, and balance the desire for market-based assessments of risk with a greater role for the government agency, such as SEC, or an independent board in defining rating agencies' responsibilities.

According to its author, this user-fee model creates additional accountability mechanisms. Users of ratings would be given enforceable rights and would require NRSROs to assume certification and mandatory reporting duties to creditors. The system would set up creditor committees that would serve as a channel for creditors to monitor ratings and assert limited rights against NRSROs. If an NRSRO breached duties owed to the creditors, the committee would serve as the representative in any potential actions and preempt actions brought by individual creditors. The model would require that all contracts with NRSROs detail duties owed to their creditors, to delineate the potential liability exposure for

---

[20]In instances in which companies fail to issue rated debt, SEC could be empowered to impose the user fee on the issuers themselves since they would be the only readily identifiable beneficiaries of information on their creditworthiness, according to the authors of this proposed model..

breach of these duties, and channel adjudication of any disputes to an SEC administrative process. For example, NRSROs could be required to certify on a quarterly basis that they exercised reasonable care in conducting due diligence of issuers' financial and nonfinancial disclosures to make accurate assessments of risk exposure. To provide NRSROs with incentives for compliance without jeopardizing their financial viability, the model would limit NRSRO financial liability to cases of gross negligence, coupled with an earnings-based cap on liability and other safeguards.

Issuer and Investor-Pays Model

This proposed model incorporates characteristics from a number of the models described earlier and leverages an existing structure as the basis for collecting and distributing ratings fees. Under the proposed issuer and investor-pays model, accredited NRSROs would be assigned to rate new issuances. Initially, all NRSROs would be placed in a continuous queue and would receive rating assignments when their respective numbers came up, unless they were unable or unwilling to rate a particular issue. In the future, ratings would be assigned based on the performances of the NRSROs, with those agencies that produced superior performance receiving more assignments. Performance would be measured as the correlation between an NRSRO's ratings and default and recovery rates on issues rated, and tracked using a common, transparent, and defensible methodology. To help ensure rigor and fairness, at least two and possibly three NRSROs would be assigned to rate each issuance.

Payments for ratings would come from a fee levied on issuers of new debt issues and investors as parties of secondary market trades. These fees would be deposited in a dedicated fund—the U.S. Ratings Fund—and would be determined and reset periodically. The periodic review would consider the historic and projected volumes of primary issuances and of secondary market trading to determine a fee that would in the aggregate allow the ratings business to attract and retain qualified individuals. This fund would be modeled after the Municipal Securities Rulemaking Board (MSRB), which is authorized to collect fees on new and secondary market municipal issues to fund its activities, and would be overseen by a governing board representing issuers, investors, rating agencies, intermediaries, and independent directors. The fees collected would be used to pay the selected accredited NRSROs for issuing each solicited rating and other necessary administrative activities such as tracking NRSRO's performance and tracking deals to be rated. The authors note that these other activities could be outsourced or performed by the U.S. Ratings Fund. The Fund also would advise SEC on the eligibility and accreditation of the NRSROs. All ratings and related research reports paid for through the U.S. Ratings Fund would be freely available to the public.

According to the authors, NRSROs would have incentives to provide accurate ratings and be objective because ratings would be monitored by a regulator and the accreditation of NRSROs would be subject to periodic renewal. The authors also note that legislation likely would be required to set up the new rating agency compensation model. Specifically, the authors said that legislation would need to enumerate the functions and the governance structure of the U.S. Ratings Fund, provide its mandate and methodology for determining the fees to be charged for ratings, and elaborate on how the new rating model would be introduced.[21]

Comment Letters to SEC Supported Implementing One Alternative Model or Enhancing Existing Rules

During debate on the Dodd-Frank Act, a system similar to the random selection model was proposed through an amendment to the Securities Exchange Act of 1934. Proposed section 939D would have added a section 15E(w) to the Exchange Act which would require SEC to establish a Credit Rating Agency Board that was a self-regulatory organization subject to SEC's oversight. The Board would determine NRSROs that are eligible to issue initial credit ratings for structured finance products and assign NRSROs to rate the issuances (NRSROs could decline). The method for selecting the qualified NRSROs would be based on a Board evaluation of alternatives designed to reduce the conflicts of interest under the issuer-pays model, including a lottery or rotational assignment system. Although the section 939D amendment was passed by the Senate, it was not included in the final legislation. However, the Dodd-

---

[21]A variant of the issuer and investor pay model—with similar features and legislative needs—is a "market pay" model concept in which the credit rating agencies would be part of a cooperative overseen by a board made up of individuals representing institutional and retail investor interests. The board's primary functions would be to approve credit rating agencies eligible to rate issuances and collect and distribute fees to the selected credit rating agencies that provided rating services. Implementation of this model would also likely require legislation; such as to enumerate the functions and the governance of the oversight board, as well as to establish the cooperative framework. Unlike the issuer and investor pay model, this variant would generate funds to pay the rating agencies' fees (and potentially board costs) by incorporating a market-wide fee into the issuances' coupon rate, i.e., a payment strip. It also differs by allowing the issuer and investors (as a group) each to select the credit rating agencies in the cooperative they would like to rate the issuances. There would be a limit to the number of rating agencies selected, potentially up to two selected by an issuer and two by the investors. As with the issuer and investor pay model, all ratings and related research would be freely available to the public.

Frank Act provides that upon completion of the section 939F study, SEC shall, as it determines is necessary or appropriate in the public interest or for the protection of investors, establish by rule a system for the assignment of NRSROs to determine the initial credit ratings and monitor the credit ratings of structured finance products in a manner that prevents the arranger from selecting the NRSRO that will determine the credit rating. In issuing any rule, the act requires SEC to give thorough consideration to the provisions of section 15E(w) of the Exchange Act, as that provision would have been added by section 939D as passed by the Senate on May 20, 2010, and SEC must implement the system described in such section 939D unless SEC determines that an alternative system would better serve the public interest and the protection of investors.

In May 2011, SEC requested that interested parties provide comments on whether any potential alternative compensation model, including four of the models we described in our 2010 report and discussed previously would provide a reasonable alternative to the section 15E(w) model in terms of objectives and goals. SEC omitted the random selection model from its request for comment because it is similar to the section 15E(w) model. As part of this solicitation of comments, SEC requested that interested parties use the evaluative framework we developed for our 2010 report to evaluate the section 15E(w) and other alternative compensation models.[22] The comment period ended in September 2011.

Our analysis of the comment letters that various market participants and observers submitted on SEC's section 939F study found that while some supported implementing the section 15E(w) model, others preferred enhancing existing SEC rules. Of the 30 comment letters submitted, our assessments found that 11 generally favored implementing an alternative compensation model, 13 opposed the implementation of an alternative compensation model, and 5 did not comment on the need for an

---

[22]We developed a framework to assist regulators and policymakers identify a model's relative strengths and weaknesses, potential trade-offs in terms of policy goals, or areas in which further elaboration or clarification would be warranted. See appendix I for more information on our evaluation framework.

alternative compensation model.[23] Sixteen comment letters either supported or made suggestions for improving existing SEC rules. None of the comment letters supported any of the other alternative compensation models described by SEC in its request for comment.[24] Only seven addressed the alternative models individually and all were critical of these alternatives.

Only the section 15E(w) model received specific support from those that supported the implementation of an alternative compensation model. Generally, these letters highlighted the need to address the conflict of interest inherent in the issuer-pays model. For example, one commenter stated that an assignment system—such as the one proposed in the model—best serves the public interest by increasing competition to allow for new NRSRO participants. The author of another comment letter stated that on balance he favored a system—such as the one proposed in the 15E(w) model—that would separate issuer payment for ratings on structured finance products from issuer selection of NRSROs.

Those opposed to the implementation of an alternative compensation model, including the section 15E(w) model, cited concerns such as replacing one set of conflicts of interest with another and raised issues about the cost of implementation. According to a few comment letters, each of the proposed models presents its own unique set of issues and often substitutes one type of conflict of interest for another. For example, one comment letter stated that each compensation model has unavoidable conflicts of interest and that none of the alternatives presented by SEC would offer practical or effective solutions to the risks of potential conflicts engendered by the issuer-pays model. Another

---

[23]One commenter submitted two comment letters, both in favor of the 15E(w) model. We counted this commenter's support only once when tallying the letters for or against the implementation of an alternative compensation model. Of the five that did not comment on the need for an alternative compensation model, three discussed the models but did not specifically comment on the need for one and two did not address the alternative compensation models. SEC staff are in the preliminary stages of analyzing the comment letters.

[24]SEC staff also interpreted one comment letter as supporting a combination of the 15E(w) model and the stand- alone model. We interpreted this to be a unique alternative compensation model and thus the letter was not showing support for any of the other alternative compensation models described by SEC in its request for comment. We described the model put forth in this comment letter earlier as the alternative user-pays model.

comment letter cited specific conflicts various market participants may have, concluding that changing "who pays" the credit rating agency will not eliminate the potential for conflicts: it will only shift the conflicts from one set of interested parties to another.[25] Comment letters also stated that some of the models would create large costs. For example, one comment letter stated that the selection board created in the section 15E(w) model would need to employ a significant staff with highly specialized skills to credibly carry out its responsibilities. Another letter described the extensive amount of infrastructure that would be needed to assess fees on each trade, such as those required by the stand-alone model.

Many of the letters opposed to the implementation of an alternative compensation model noted the need for the improvement of existing rules. For example, multiple comment letters suggested that SEC's rule 17g-5, which is designed to make it more difficult for issuers to exert influence over NRSROs by making the information necessary to rate the issuance available to all NRSROs, addresses many of the concerns that the alternative compensation models propose to address. They added that this rule could be improved by increasing the percent of "free peeks" an NRSRO would be allowed before having to produce an unsolicited rating.[26] Others advocated the removal of the requirement entirely or replacing the "unsolicited rating requirement" with a requirement that ratings agencies provide a specified number of "rating commentaries or other credit quality statements." Finally, some advocated for the

---

[25]Similarly, in our 2010 report we noted that the subscrber-pays model also is subject to conflicts of interest because the investors could influence the NRSRO to upgrade or downgrade securities investors were holding to their advantage. For example, subscribers may want to hold only investment-grade securities because their investment guidelines require this. An upgrade to investment grade would allow subscrbers to hold that security. See GAO-10-782.

[26]Rule 17g-5 requires an NRSRO hired to determine initial credit ratings for structured finance products to maintain a password-protected Internet website containing a list of each such structured finance product for which it currently is in the process of determining an initial credit rating. The rule is designed to make it more difficult for arrangers to exert influence over the NRSRO they hire because any inappropriate rating could be exposed to the market through the unsolicited ratings issued by NRSROs not hired to rate the structured finance product. However, the rule limits the number of times an NRSRO can access the information without having to produce its own credit ratings. An NRSRO that accesses information 10 or more times during the calendar year must produce a credit rating for at least 10 percent of the issues for which it accessed information. *See* 17 C.F.R. § 240.17g-5(a)(3).

information provided to the selected NRSRO to be made more broadly available, particularly to investors.

SEC Is Implementing the Dodd-Frank Act and Reviewing Its Authority to Implement the Alternative Compensation Models

The Dodd-Frank Act requires SEC to take a number of actions regarding its oversight of NRSROs including issuing a number of rulemakings, establishing an Office of Credit Ratings, and studying, among other things, the feasibility of an assignment system for the ratings of structured finance products and alternative means for compensating NRSROs. As part of this study, SEC has solicited comment on its authority to implement the alternative compensation models.

SEC Has Taken a Number of Steps to Implement Dodd-Frank Act Requirements

Since the enactment of the Dodd-Frank Act in July 2010, SEC has taken a number of steps to implement the parts of the act pertaining to NRSROs. Of the 15 requirements for SEC contained in Title IX of the Dodd-Frank Act, 9 require SEC to issue rules. As of January 2012, SEC has adopted three final rules that implement all or part of certain requirements and proposed rules to implement the remaining requirements. Specifically, SEC has adopted rules removing the exemption for NRSROs from the Fair Disclosure Rule; requiring NRSROs to include a report accompanying a credit rating for an asset-backed security describing representations, warranties, and enforcement mechanisms available to investors; and removing references to NRSRO credit ratings from certain securities registration requirements. SEC has also proposed a number of amendments to existing rules or new rules to implement the remainder of the Dodd-Frank Act requirements applicable to NRSROs. Table 1 provides a summary of these proposals.

Table 1: Summary of Existing Rules, Proposed Amendments, and Proposed New Rules Applicable to NRSROs and Promulgated under the Dodd-Frank Act, as of January 2012

Rule number	Summary of existing rules	Summary of proposed amendments to existing rules	Summary of proposed new rules
Rule 17g-1	Prescribes how an NRSRO must apply to be registered with SEC, keep its registration up-to-date, and comply with the statutory requirement to furnish SEC with an annual certification. Specifically, all of these actions must be accomplished by furnishing SEC with information on a Form NRSRO. As part of registration, NRSROs must disclose certain performance statistics and general descriptions of their ratings processes and methodologies.	Revises instructions to exhibit 1 of Form NRSRO to standardize the manner in which NRSROs present performance measurement statistics and define important terms such as "default." Requires that all exhibits (1-9) to Form NRSRO be made available to the public from an easily accessible portion of the NRSRO's website.	N/A
Rule 17g-2	Requires an NRSRO to make and retain certain types of business records and disclose certain ratings history data.	Updates rule to include new record-keeping requirements resulting from amendments to other rules or new rules. For example, to identify the internal control structure, an NRSRO must document the structure in a record that must be retained. Enhances ratings history disclosures to require NRSROs to disclose the rating histories for any credit rating that was outstanding as of June 26, 2007, and repeals a rule requiring issuer-pays rating agencies to disclose a random 10 percent sample of outstanding ratings in each class of ratings in which they have more than 500 issuer-paid ratings. Also, it would move the provisions of the 100 percent rule to 17g-7.	N/A
Rule 17g-3	Requires an NRSRO to furnish SEC with four, or in some cases five, financial reports annually. The first report requires the submission of audited financial statements. The remaining reports are unaudited. Also requires the NRSRO to provide SEC with an unaudited report of the number of credit rating actions during the fiscal year in each class of credit rating for which it is registered.	Requires an NRSRO to file an unaudited report on the NRSRO's internal control structure with its annual submission of reports. The proposal also requires a statement signed by the CEO or person performing similar functions, attesting that the report fairly presents a description of the responsibilities of management in establishing and maintaining an effective internal control structure.	N/A

Rule number	Summary of existing rules	Summary of proposed amendments to existing rules	Summary of proposed new rules
Rule 17g-4	Prescribes minimal requirements for the policies and procedures that registered NRSROs are required to establish, maintain, and enforce to address specific areas in which material, nonpublic information could be inappropriately disclosed or used.	N/A	N/A
Rule 17g-5	Prohibits certain actions that constitute an impermissible conflict of interest and prescribes requirements to manage other inherent conflicts of interest. Requires an NRSRO hired by an arranger to rate a structured finance product to obtain representation from the arranger that it will provide information it has been given to the nonhired NRSROs.	Identifies a new prohibited conflict, sets forth the finding the Commission would need to make to grant a small NRSRO an exemption from the prohibition, and sets forth the standard for suspending or revoking an NRSRO registration for a violation of any rule under section 15E(h). Includes a new absolute prohibition on an NRSRO issuing or maintaining a credit rating where a person within the NRSRO who participates in the sales or marketing of a product or service of the NRSRO also participates in determining or monitoring the credit rating, or developing or approving procedures or methodologies used for determining the credit rating. SEC can determine that separation of production and sales and marketing is not appropriate for small NRSROs and waive the requirement for these NRSROs.	N/A
Rule 17g-6	Prohibits any act or practice by an NRSRO that SEC determines to be unfair, abusive, or coercive.	N/A	N/A
Rule 17g-7	N/A	N/A	Requires an NRSRO to include in a report accompanying a credit rating for an offering of asset-backed securities describing the representations, warranties, and enforcement mechanisms available to investors; and how they differ from representations, warranties, and enforcement mechanisms in issuances of similar securities. Also information on any preliminary ratings. *(Adopted Jan. 20, 2011.)* Enhances the 100 percent rule to require disclosure of information about all outstanding credit ratings in each class and subclass of credit ratings for which the NRSRO is

Rule number	Summary of existing rules	Summary of proposed amendments to existing rules	Summary of proposed new rules
			registered, within certain prescribed time frames. The rule would apply to any credit rating that was outstanding as of June 26, 2007, but the rating histories disclosed for these credit ratings would not need to include information about actions taken before June 26, 2007.
Rule 17g-8	N/A	N/A	Requires the NRSRO to establish, maintain, and enforce policies and procedures reasonably designed to ensure that in any case in which an employee of a person, issuer, sponsor, etc. subject to a credit rating was employed by the NRSRO and participated in any capacity in determining the credit rating for that person during the 1-year period preceding the date an action was taken on that rating the NRSRO will conduct a review to determine if there were any conflicts of interest.

If a conflict is found, the NRSRO shall

(1) immediately place the credit rating on credit watch, including providing users of credit ratings with immediate notice.

(2) promptly determine if the credit rating must be revised.

(3) promptly publish a new rating or reaffirm the existing rating.

Requires NRSROs to ensure that credit ratings are determined using procedures and methodologies, including qualitative and quantitative data and models, which are approved by the board of the NRSRO, or a body performing a function similar to that of a board. It also would require an NRSRO to ensure that when material changes are made to credit rating procedures and methodologies, to the extent that changes are made to credit rating surveillance procedures and methodologies, the changes are applied to then-current credit ratings by the NRSRO within a reasonable time period. |

Rule number	Summary of existing rules	Summary of proposed amendments to existing rules	Summary of proposed new rules
Rule 17g-9	N/A	N/A	Requires that any person employed by an NRSRO to perform credit ratings meets standards of training, experience, and competence and is tested for knowledge of the credit rating process. The proposed rule also identifies certain factors that an NSRO must consider in designing its standards and two factors that must be incorporated into the standards.
Rule 17g-10	N/A	N/A	Provides that the signed written certifications of providers of third-party due diligence services required must be made on Form ABS Due Diligence-E15.
Regulation FD	N/A	Removes the specific exemption that allowed an issuer to not make public the disclosure of material nonpublic information if the only disclosure of that information is made to a credit rating agency that makes its credit ratings publicly available (adopted September 29, 2011).	N/A
Rules 134, 138, 139, 168, Form S-3, Form S-4, Form F-3 and Form F-4	N/A	Remove references to credit ratings (adopted July 27, 2011).	N/A
Rule 2a-7, Form N-MFP, Forms N-1A, N-2, and N-3	N/A	Remove references to credit ratings or eliminate the disclosure of credit ratings (proposed March 3, 2011).	N/A
Rule 6a-5	N/A	Replaces references to credit ratings with a new standard of creditworthiness. Under the new standard, a security is elig ble for investment by a specific type of company if the board of directors or members of the company determine that the debt security is (i) subject to no greater than moderate credit risk and (ii) sufficiently liquid that the security can be sold at or near its carrying value within a reasonably short period of time (proposed March 3, 2011).	N/A

Rule number	Summary of existing rules	Summary of proposed amendments to existing rules	Summary of proposed new rules
Rules 15c3-1, 15c3-3, 17a-4; Rules 101 and 102 of Regulation M and 10b-10 and Form X-17A-5 Part IIB.	N/A	Remove references to credit ratings and in certain cases substitute alternative standards of creditworthiness (proposed April 27, 2011).	N/A

Source: GAO summary of SEC Proposed Rule Release.

Note: All of the proposed amendments to existing rules and new rules were proposed on May 18, 2011, and published in the Federal Register on June 8, 2011, unless otherwise noted in the table. According to its website, SEC plans to finalize the remaining proposed rules and amendments between January and June 2012. However, SEC proposed rules for the removal of statutory references to credit ratings from specific laws, and regulations require SEC to coordinate with other federal regulators. Thus, it is unclear when SEC may adopt final rules pertaining to other rules and regulations this issue.

In addition to its work on NRSRO oversight rules, SEC continues to work on other Dodd-Frank Act requirements related to NRSROs. These requirements include completing four studies on various aspects of the credit rating industry.[27] As of January 2012, SEC has completed one of the four studies and issued a report which provided a summary of SEC regulations requiring the use of an assessment of the creditworthiness of a security or money market instrument and any references to or requirements in such regulations regarding credit ratings. According to SEC's website, SEC plans to complete two of the remaining three studies by July 2012; the completion date for the other study has yet to be determined.

---

[27] Section 939A requires SEC to review any regulation that requires the use of an assessment of the creditworthiness of a security and any references to or requirements in such regulations regarding credit ratings. SEC provided this report to Congress on July 21, 2011. Section 939C requires SEC to study the independence of NRSROs and how the independence of NRSROs affects the ratings issued by the NRSROs. This report is to be completed not later than 3 years after the date of enactment of the Dodd-Frank Act. As described previously, section 939(h) requires SEC to study, among other things, the feasibility and desirability of standardizing credit rating terminology, standardizing market stress conditions under which ratings are evaluated, and requiring a quantitative correspondence between credit ratings and a range of default probabilities and loss expectations under standardized conditions of economic stress. This study was to be completed no later than 1 year after the date of enactment of the Dodd-Frank Act. Section 939F requires SEC to study the rating process for structured finance products and associated conflicts of interest, the feasibility of an assignment system, metrics to determine the accuracy of ratings, and alternative means for compensating NRSROs. This report is to be completed not later than 24 months after the date of enactment of the Dodd-Frank Act.

Finally, the Dodd-Frank Act requires SEC to establish an Office of Credit Ratings and complete annual examinations of each NRSRO. Once established, this office will be responsible for administering the rules of SEC in certain areas, promoting accuracy in credit ratings, and conducting annual examinations of each NRSRO.[28] Although the office has yet to be established, NRSRO examination staff from SEC's Office of Compliance Inspections and Examinations (OCIE), staff from OCIE's investment adviser/investment company and broker-dealer examination groups, and NRSRO specialists from SEC's Division of Trading and Markets recently completed the first cycle of annual examinations of each NRSRO as required by the Dodd-Frank Act. SEC made public a staff report summarizing the examinations in September 2011.[29] According to this report, limited SEC resources required that this year's examinations focus on reviewing the areas mandated by section 15E(p)(3)(B)— specifically, whether the NRSRO conducts business in accordance with its policies, procedures, and rating methodologies; management of conflicts of interest; implementation of ethics policies; internal supervisory controls; governance; activities of the designated compliance officer; processing of complaints; and NRSRO's policies governing the post-employment activities of former staff of the NRSRO. The report summarized the examination staff's notable observations and concerns and the recommendations the staff made to each NRSRO about these observations and concerns related to the following required review areas: conducting business in accordance with policies, procedures, and methodologies; management of conflicts of interest; internal supervisory controls; and designated compliance officer activities. The report notes that, as of the date of the report, SEC had not determined that any finding constituted a "material regulatory deficiency," but noted that the Commission may do so in the future. The staff also made the observation that NRSROs appear to be trending even more toward employing the issuer-pays business model, noting that two of the subscriber-pays

---

[28]According to SEC, in order to establish this office in fiscal year 2011, SEC needed approval to reprogram funds for this purpose from both the House and Senate Appropriations Subcommittees on Financial Services and General Government but was not able to reach agreement with the subcommittees. SEC maintains that with the enactment of SEC's fiscal year 2012 regular appropriation, the SEC can now establish the office.

[29]See SEC, *2011 Summary Report of Commission Staff's Examinations of Each Nationally Recognized Statistical Rating Organization, As Required by Section 15(p)(3)(C) of the Securities Exchange Act of 1934* (Washington, D.C.: September 2011).

NRSROs recently have taken steps to focus more on issuer-pays business, particularly with respect to ratings of asset-back securities.

SEC Is Conducting Its Required Study of Alternative Compensation Models, but Has Yet to Talk to the Models' Authors

Section 939F of the Dodd-Frank Act requires that SEC conduct a study that addresses, among other things, the feasibility of establishing a system in which a public or private utility or an SRO assigns NRSROs to determine the credit ratings of structured finance products. SEC's report on the study, due by July 21, 2012, must include any recommendations for regulatory or statutory changes that SEC determines should be made to implement the findings of the study. As part of this study, SEC solicited comment on its authority to implement various alternative compensation models. According to SEC staff, the staff is reviewing the comment letters received and is evaluating authority issues.

Section 939F requires that, after submission of the report to Congress resulting from the study, SEC shall, by rule, as the SEC determines is necessary or appropriate in the public interest or for the protection of investors, establish a system for the assignment of NRSROs to determine the initial credit ratings of structured finance products, in a manner that prevents the issuer, sponsor, or underwriter of the structured finance product from selecting the NRSRO that will determine the initial credit ratings and monitor such credit ratings. In issuing any rule, SEC is required to give through consideration to the provisions of section 15E(w) of the Securities Exchange Act of 1934, as that provision would have been added by section 939D of H.R. 4173 (111[h] Congress), as passed by the Senate on May 20, 2010, and shall implement the system described in such section 939D unless the Commission determines that an alternative system would better serve the public interest and the protection of investors. The need for any statutory changes likely will depend on the system that SEC decides to implement. Therefore, obtaining as complete information on the models as available, such as by consulting with the models' authors, will be important for SEC to fully assess each model in order to make its decision and any recommendations for statutory changes SEC determines should be made to implement its findings.

As part of its request for public comment in connection with its study, SEC requested comment on whether the securities laws provide SEC with authority to implement the 15E(w) system and the four other models it outlined. In particular, SEC asked for comment on whether, in terms of legal feasibility, the role of SEC in overseeing the Credit Rating Agency Board raised legal issues. Few comment letters directly addressed SEC's questions concerning its authority to implement one or any of the alternative compensation models outlined in its request for comment. However, a few of the comment letters discussed potential legal questions surrounding the implementation of or rulemaking for specific aspects of certain models, or general constitutional questions. For instance, two commenters argued that in their view, NRSRO ratings legally are viewed as opinions and may not be subject to being proven true or false. Thus any system that utilizes the accuracy of ratings as criteria to determine which NRSROs would be eligible to rate certain categories of securities—such as the 15E(w) system—may face legal challenges.[30] One comment letter also argued that any system aimed at defining "quality" ratings could run afoul of Section 15E(c)(2) of the Exchange Act, which provides that SEC may not "regulate the substance of credit ratings or the procedures and methodologies by which any NRSRO determines credit ratings."[31] The letter states that any decision by SEC that an NRSRO's ratings (and, by extension, the criteria and methodologies by which those ratings were formed) lack "quality" and therefore must be changed to maintain participation in the proposed system could well violate this provision. In addition, three comment letters raised constitutional questions. Two comment letters questioned how certain of the alternative models might affect an NRSRO's right to form and publish opinions under the First Amendment. Another questioned the ability of the government to force one private party to deal with another private party of the government's choosing in a private business transaction, which the commenter argues would occur if SEC implemented the section 15E(w) model.

The model authors also hold varying opinions on the extent to which statutory changes would be necessary to implement their alternative compensation model. For example, in their paper introducing the model and in our discussions with them, the authors of the proposed issuer and investor-pays model discussed that they anticipate that legislation would likely be required to implement their proposed model. Specifically, authors of the model stated that legislation would likely be necessary to establish the self-regulatory organization and provide it with the authority to create a fund to collect fees and impose data collection requirements on

---

[30]Currently, no widely accepted measure of ratings accuracy exists. According to SEC staff and comment letters, developing such a measure would be difficult.

[31]15 U.S.C. § 78o-7(c)(2).

issuances, the governance structure of the fund, the methodology for determining fees, an initial rotating system of assignments of issues to be rated, and broad parameters for incentive compensation. Alternatively, the author of the proposed investor-owned credit rating agency model we interviewed believes that current law, even before the Dodd-Frank Act was passed, provides SEC with the authority to implement the model as a means of managing the conflicts of interest generated by the issuer-pays model.[32] Specifically, the author points to sections 15E(h)(2) of the Exchange Act, which grants SEC the authority to issue rules to prohibit, or require the management and disclosure of, any conflicts of interest relating to the issuance of credit ratings by the NRSRO.[33] This includes the authority to issue rules relating to the manner in which an NRSRO is compensated by the issuer for issuing credit ratings. The author also stated that section 15E(i)(1), which provides that SEC shall issue rules to prohibit any act or practice relating to the issuance of credit ratings by an NRSRO that SEC determines to be unfair, coercive, or abusive provides additional statutory authority for the implementation of the investor-owned credit rating agency model.[34] As previously discussed, SEC has not spoken to the authors of the proposed models to solicit additional details about their models—information that could help inform SEC's analysis of the alternative compensation models and its report to Congress containing any recommendations for regulatory or statutory changes that it determines should be made to implement the findings of its study.

Conclusion

In recent years, academic researchers and industry experts have begun to develop a number of alternative compensation models for credit rating agencies in response to concerns about conflict of interest, ratings integrity, and competition. As of January 2012, none of these models have been fully developed, and given that NRSROs continue to primarily use the issuer-pays, and to a lesser extent, the subscriber-pays models, the use of any alternative model or models would likely have to be at the

---

[32]However, one paper we reviewed noted that significant legal difficulty arises with proposals to mandate behavior by investors—two of the models require the users of credit ratings to pay a fee—because SEC and other securities regulators have no delegated power over investors as a group. *See* John C. Coffee, Jr., *Ratings Reform: The Good, The Bad, and The Ugly*, 1 Harv. Bus. L. Rev. 231, 259 n.72 (2011).

[33]15 U.S.C. § 78o-7(h)(2).

[34]15 U.S.C. § 78o-7(i)(1).

direction of SEC or Congress. As directed by section 939F of the Dodd-Frank Act, SEC is currently studying, among other things, alternative means for compensating NRSROs that would create incentives for accurate credit ratings. As part of its study, SEC solicited public comment on various alternative compensation models and whether it has sufficient authority to implement these models. Few of the comment letters SEC received specifically addressed the alternative models or SEC's authority to implement them, and only one of the model authors submitted a comment letter to SEC. Currently, the staff is reviewing the comment letters received and evaluating authority issues, however the extent to which SEC's existing authorities would allow it to implement any of the alternative models by rule largely will depend on the system selected. As part of its 939F study, SEC has not met with the authors of the various alternative compensation models to discuss the models in greater detail. Doing so could help ensure that SEC has thoroughly explored all of the available options in sufficient enough detail to adequately consider them. Without consulting the authors to gain a comprehensive understanding of the proposed models, SEC may not have complete information available to be able to fully determine the authorities it may need to implement a particular model.

Recommendation for Executive Action

As SEC continues to study the various alternative means for compensating NRSROs, as well as determine whether a system for the assignment of initial credit ratings for structured finance products is necessary or appropriate in the public interest or for the protection of investors, SEC should consult with the authors to better ensure it has all available information on the models to make its decision, and include in its report to Congress any recommendations for statutory changes the SEC determines should be made to implement the findings of the study.

Agency Comments and Our Evaluation

We provided a draft of the report to the Chairman of the Securities and Exchange Commission (SEC) for her review and comment. SEC's written comments are reprinted in appendix II. We also received technical comments from SEC that were incorporated, where appropriate. In its written comments, SEC agreed with our recommendation. In describing its statutory responsibilities and the steps it has taken to implement them, SEC noted that as it continues working on its 939F study, the Commission staff will seek to consult further with the parties that have proposed alternative compensation models for NRSROs to better ensure that the Commission has all available information on such models.

We are sending copies of this report to SEC, appropriate congressional committees and members, and other interested parties. The report also is available at no charge on the GAO website at http://www.gao.gov.

If you or your staffs have any questions about this report, please contact me at (202) 512-8678 or clowersa@gao.gov. Contact points for our Offices of Congressional Relations and Public Affairs may be found on the last page of this report. GAO staff who made major contributions to this report are listed in appendix III.

A. Nicole Clowers
Director,
Financial Markets and
    Community Investment Issues

Appendix I: Framework to Evaluate Alternative Compensation Models

To assist Congress and others in assessing these proposed alternative compensation models, we developed an evaluative framework for our 2010 report with seven factors that any compensation model should address to be fully effective. The framework can help identify a model's relative strengths and weaknesses, potential trade-offs (in terms of policy goals), or areas in which further elaboration or clarification would be warranted using the following factors:

- **Independence.** The ability for the compensation model to mitigate conflicts of interest inherent between the entity paying for the rating and the nationally recognized statistical rating organization (NRSRO).

- **Accountability.** The ability of the compensation model to promote NRSROs' responsibility for the accuracy and timeliness of their ratings.

- **Competition.** The extent to which the compensation model creates an environment in which NRSROs compete for customers by producing higher-quality ratings at competitive prices.

- **Transparency.** The accessibility, usability, and clarity of the compensation model and the dissemination of information on the model to market participants.[1]

- **Feasibility.** The ease and simplicity with which the compensation model can be implemented in the securities market.

- **Market acceptance and choice.** The willingness of the securities market to accept the compensation model, the ratings produced under that model, and any new market players established by the compensation model.

- **Oversight.** The evaluation of the model to help ensure it works as intended.

See GAO-10-782 for more detailed descriptions of the seven factors.

---

[1]Transparency in this context does not refer to the transparency or disclosure regime of the NRSROs but is specific to the transparency of the model.

Appendix II: Comments from the Securities and Exchange Commission

UNITED STATES
SECURITIES AND EXCHANGE COMMISSION
WASHINGTON, DC 20549

DIVISION OF
TRADING AND MARKETS

January 11, 2011

A. Nicole Clowers
Director
Financial Markets and Community Investment Issues
Government Accountability Office
441 G Street, NW
Washington, DC 20548

Dear Ms. Clowers:

Thank you for the opportunity to comment on the Government Accountability Office (GAO) draft report entitled *Credit Rating Agencies: Alternative Compensation Models for Nationally Recognized Statistical Rating Organizations* (Draft Report), a report required under section 939D of the Wall Street Reform and Consumer Protection Act (Dodd-Frank Act).[1] This letter supplements the technical comments on the Draft Report we have provided the GAO telephonically and by email.

The Draft Report discusses: (1) alternatives for compensating nationally recognized statistical rating organizations (NRSROs); (2) the Commission's actions to implement the Dodd-Frank Act requirements specific to the Commission's oversight of NRSROs; and (3) the Commission's authority to implement an alternative compensation model under current laws. The Commission has been analyzing alternative compensation models for NRSROs for several years. For example, in April 2009, the Commission hosted a roundtable discussion regarding its oversight of credit rating agencies. At this roundtable, proponents of a variety of alternative NRSRO compensation models were given the opportunity to present their ideas. Subsequent to the roundtable, Commission staff contacted a number of the presenters on this topic to gain further insights into their ideas.

The Dodd-Frank Act enacted in July 2010 required both the GAO and the Commission to perform further work on alternative compensation models. Specifically, section 939D of the Dodd-Frank Act requires the GAO to conduct a study on alternative means for compensating NRSROs that could create incentives to provide more accurate credit ratings, including any statutory changes that would be required to facilitate the use of an alternative means of compensation. Section 939D further provides that the GAO, not later than 18 months after

---

[1] Any views expressed in this letter and views of the Commission staff reflected in the Draft Report are those of the Commission staff interviewed by the GAO and do not necessarily reflect the views of the Commission, the individual Commissioners, or other Commission staff.

enactment of the Dodd-Frank Act, shall submit to the Committee on Banking, Housing, and Urban Affairs of the Senate and the Committee on Financial Services of the House of Representatives a report on the results of the study, including recommendations, if any, for providing incentives to credit rating agencies to improve the credit rating process. The Draft Report is the result of this statutory requirement.

Section 939F of the Dodd-Frank Act requires the Commission to conduct a study addressing four areas: (1) the credit rating process for structured finance products and the conflicts of interest associated with the issuer-pay and the subscriber-pay models; (2) the feasibility of establishing a system in which a public or private utility or an SRO assigns NRSROs to determine the credit ratings for structured finance products, including an assessment of potential mechanisms for determining fees for NRSROs for structured finance products and appropriate methods for paying fees to NRSROs to rate structured finance products; (3) the range of metrics one could use to determine the accuracy of credit ratings for structured finance products; and (4) alternative means for compensating NRSROs that would create incentives for accurate credit ratings for structured finance products. In addition, section 939F provides that the Commission must submit to the Committee on Banking, Housing, and Urban Affairs of the Senate and the Committee on Financial Services of the House of Representatives, not later than 24 months after the date of enactment of the Dodd-Frank Act, a report containing: (1) the findings of a study on matters related to assigning credit ratings for structured finance products; and (2) any recommendations for regulatory or statutory changes that the Commission determines should be made to implement the findings of the study.

Section 939F further provides that, after submission of the report to Congress resulting from the study, the Commission shall, by rule, as the Commission determines is necessary or appropriate in the public interest or for the protection of investors, establish a system for the assignment of NRSROs to determine the initial credit ratings of structured finance products, in a manner that prevents the issuer, sponsor, or underwriter of the structured finance product from selecting the NRSRO that will determine the initial credit ratings and monitor such credit ratings. In issuing any rule, the Commission is required to give thorough consideration to the provisions of section 15E(w) of the Securities Exchange Act of 1934, as that provision would have been added by section 939D of H.R. 4173 (111th Congress), as passed by the Senate on May 20, 2010, and shall implement the system described in such section 939D unless the Commission determines that an alternative system would better serve the public interest and the protection of investors.

As noted in the Draft Report, in May 2011 the Commission issued a comprehensive solicitation of comment to assist in conducting the study required by section 939F. The Commission gave the public 120 days to comment on the solicitation in order to provide all interested parties with ample opportunity to submit thoughtful comments. In soliciting comment, the Commission was greatly assisted by the framework the GAO developed for analyzing alternative compensation models in its report entitled: *Securities and Exchange Commission: Action Needed to Improve Rating Agency Registration Program and Performance Related Disclosures*, GAO Report 10-782 (September 2010). The GAO's Framework consists of a seven

A. Nicole Clowers
January 11, 2012
Page 3

factor test to use in evaluating such models.[2] The Commission, in its solicitation of comment, asked interested parties to analyze various identified compensation models using the GAO's framework. The Commission received approximately 30 comments and is now working on the study, taking the comments received into consideration. In addition, consistent with the recommendation in the Draft Report, the Commission staff will seek to consult further with the parties that have proposed alternative compensation models for NRSROs to better ensure that the Commission has all available information on such models.

On behalf of the Commission staff, we thank the GAO staff for the opportunity to review and comment on the Draft Report before it is issued in its final form.

Sincerely,

Robert W. Cook
Director

---

[2] The seven factors are: (1) independence (the ability for the compensation model to mitigate conflicts of interest inherent between the entity paying for the rating and the NRSRO); (2) accountability (the ability of the compensation model to promote NRSRO responsibility for the accuracy and timeliness of their ratings); (3) competition (the extent to which the compensation model creates an environment in which NRSROs compete for customers by producing higher-quality ratings at competitive prices); (4) transparency (the accessibility, usability, and clarity of the compensation model and the dissemination of information on the model to market participants); (5) feasibility (the simplicity and ease with which the compensation model can be implemented in the securities market); (6) market acceptance and choice (the willingness of the securities market to accept the compensation model, the ratings produced under that model, and any new market players established by the compensation model); and (7) oversight (the evaluation of the model to help ensure it works as intended).

Appendix III: GAO Contact and Staff Acknowledgments

GAO Contact	A. Nicole Clowers, (202) 512-8678 or clowersa@gao.gov
Staff Acknowledgments	In addition to the individual named above, Karen Tremba (Assistant Director), Rachel DeMarcus, Patrick Dynes, Matthew Keeler, Patricia Moye, Barbara Roesmann, and Jessica Sandler made key contributions to this report.

GAO's Mission	The Government Accountability Office, the audit, evaluation, and investigative arm of Congress, exists to support Congress in meeting its constitutional responsibilities and to help improve the performance and accountability of the federal government for the American people. GAO examines the use of public funds; evaluates federal programs and policies; and provides analyses, recommendations, and other assistance to help Congress make informed oversight, policy, and funding decisions. GAO's commitment to good government is reflected in its core values of accountability, integrity, and reliability.
Obtaining Copies of GAO Reports and Testimony	The fastest and easiest way to obtain copies of GAO documents at no cost is through GAO's website (www.gao.gov). Each weekday afternoon, GAO posts on its website newly released reports, testimony, and correspondence. To have GAO e-mail you a list of newly posted products, go to www.gao.gov and select "E-mail Updates."
Order by Phone	The price of each GAO publication reflects GAO's actual cost of production and distribution and depends on the number of pages in the publication and whether the publication is printed in color or black and white. Pricing and ordering information is posted on GAO's website, http://www.gao.gov/ordering.htm.

Place orders by calling (202) 512-6000, toll free (866) 801-7077, or TDD (202) 512-2537.

Orders may be paid for using American Express, Discover Card, MasterCard, Visa, check, or money order. Call for additional information. |
| **Connect with GAO** | Connect with GAO on Facebook, Flickr, Twitter, and YouTube. Subscribe to our RSS Feeds or E-mail Updates. Listen to our Podcasts. Visit GAO on the web at www.gao.gov. |
| **To Report Fraud, Waste, and Abuse in Federal Programs** | Contact:

Website: www.gao.gov/fraudnet/fraudnet.htm
E-mail: fraudnet@gao.gov
Automated answering system: (800) 424-5454 or (202) 512-7470 |
| **Congressional Relations** | Katherine Siggerud, Managing Director, siggerudk@gao.gov, (202) 512-4400, U.S. Government Accountability Office, 441 G Street NW, Room 7125 Washington, DC 20548 |
| **Public Affairs** | Chuck Young, Managing Director, youngc1@gao.gov, (202) 512-4800 U.S. Government Accountability Office, 441 G Street NW, Room 7149 Washington, DC 20548 |

www.ingramcontent.com/pod-product-compliance
Lightning Source LLC
Chambersburg PA
CBHW080926290526

45795CB00007BA/2672